Alphabet Chart

A B C D E F
G H I J K L M
N O P Q R S T
U V W X Y Z

HOW TO USE
THIS ALPHABET CHART

This alphabet chart is a reference guide for your child to use and refer to throughout the workbook. It will help your child with the sequencing, recall, and identification of the letters he or she is learning. Do not hesitate to refer to this chart as you move through the exercises. It is good practice for your child to see the letters in relation to one another in their normal place in the alphabet. Seeing letters in this context helps to reinforce your child's learning.

Once your child has become more familiar with the letters, you can use the chart to play letter games with him or her. For example, ask your child, "Can you find the J?" If necessary, you can provide helpful hints, such as "It is in the second row." Once your child is ready, increase the difficulty level of the games, asking such questions as, "Can you find the letter that is after I and before K?"

HELPING YOUR CHILD LEARN AND SUCCEED

Letter Recognition Workbook

UPPERCASE AND LOWERCASE LETTERS

By
Melissa Del'Homme, Ph.D.

Illustrated by
Kelly McMahon

LOWELL HOUSE JUVENILE

LOS ANGELES

NTC/Contemporary Publishing Group

About the Author
Melissa Del'Homme, Ph.D., earned her Doctorate in Educational Psychology with a focus on special education and developmental psychology from UCLA. She has ten years experience as an educational and behavioral program specialist, consulting with parents, teachers, school psychologists, and special educators on appropriate educational and behavioral interventions for children. Melissa also conducts research on learning and behavioral problems of children and has published several articles in this area.

Published by Lowell House
A division of NTC/Contemporary Publishing Group, Inc.
4255 West Touhy Avenue, Lincolnwood (Chicago), Illinois 60712 U.S.A.

Copyright © 2000, 1999 by NTC/Contemporary Publishing Group, Inc.
All rights reserved. No part of this book may be reproduced, stored in a retrieval system, or transmitted in any form or by any means, electronic, mechanical, photocopying, recording, or otherwise, without the prior permission of NTC/Contemporary Publishing Group, Inc.

> **This title is reproducible for classroom use only. It is not to be reproduced for an entire school or school system.**

Managing Director and Publisher: Jack Artenstein
Director of Publishing Services: Rena Copperman
Editorial Director: Brenda Pope-Ostrow
Director of Art Production: Bret Perry
Senior Educational Editor: Linda Gorman
Designer: Treesha Runnells

Lowell House books can be purchased at special discounts when ordered in bulk for premiums and special sales. Please contact Customer Service at:
NTC/Contemporary Publishing Group
4255 W. Touhy Avenue
Lincolnwood, IL 60712
1-800-323-4900

Printed and bound in the United States of America

ISBN: 0-7373-0455-3

OH 10 9 8 7 6 5 4 3 2 1

PARENT'S AND TEACHER'S NOTE

Children sometimes have trouble acquiring certain fundamental academic skills. This may be due to a variety of factors, such as:
- lack of interest
- limited attention span or distractibility
- lack of exposure to school readiness activities
- difficulty processing or interpreting written material
- memory and retention problems
- difficulty transferring or applying new skills to other situations

Children experiencing any of these difficulties can benefit from more focused and intensive instruction. **TUTOR BOOKS** are a fun, effective, and engaging way of providing this specialized teaching to children.

TUTOR BOOKS are unique in that each workbook addresses one specific educational skill. Unlike other workbooks, which attempt to encompass a wide variety of skills, these workbooks provide more focused and in-depth instruction in specific skills. In addition, by providing frequent practice, repetition, and review, **TUTOR BOOKS** offer your child more opportunities to improve his or her ability to recall and retain information.

TUTOR BOOKS also improve your child's ability to learn by:
- providing clear and simple instructions to improve comprehension
- eliminating unnecessary details to decrease distractions
- including models and examples to appeal to visual learners
- supplying additional nonworkbook activities to improve generalization of newly learned skills

Written and endorsed by experts in the field of education, these workbooks provide the level of support necessary to help your child successfully achieve his or her educational goals.

HOW TO USE

In order to get the most out of this **LETTER RECOGNITION WORKBOOK,** set aside an uninterrupted block of time—whether it's ten minutes or a half an hour—to work with your child on the activities. Be sure to choose a time when your child is alert and available for learning. Then find an area that is as free from noise and diversions as possible. This is especially important for children who are easily distracted.

Approach the workbook activities in a fun and gamelike manner. It is not "time to work on letters," but rather "time to play our letter games." This will help set a positive mood for your child, decreasing the likelihood that he or she will be turned off to these educational activities.

Work through the activities in consecutive order, as the skills build upon one another. If you see that your child is losing interest, stop. One page a day may be your child's limit. That's fine. It is important not to push him or her to go on. Remember, these activities should be fun for your child.

Keep a pack of crayons with you while working on the activities. Some pages call for your child to use color to help him or her learn. It is best not to interrupt the exercises to fetch a needed manipulative. This may cause your child's attention to wander or concentration to lessen. Also, having the crayons near you will help your child learn his or her colors while completing the main academic exercise.

While positive reinforcement is important for all children, it is absolutely key for a child who is easily frustrated, discouraged, or experiencing low self-esteem due to repeated failure in academic tasks. Periodically praise your child for his or her efforts. This will keep the mood upbeat and fun, as well as ensure that the next activity time will be met with a positive, excited response.

Use your daily routine to review the concepts your child has learned. For example, if your child has been practicing identifying certain letters, ask him or her to identify those letters in other contexts, like in magazines and newspapers, or on billboards and street signs. This will reinforce the material learned, as well as improve your child's ability to retain and recall information.

KID'S NOTE

The letters of the alphabet come in two sizes: large and small. The large letters are called **uppercase,** or **capital** letters. The small letters are called **lowercase** letters.

Here is how the letter A looks in uppercase and lowercase.

uppercase   lowercase

The first half of this book is about uppercase letters. Look for the color alphabet chart showing uppercase letters at the front of this book. The second half of this book is about lowercase letters. You will find the color alphabet chart showing lowercase letters at the back of this book. Are you ready? Let's start learning the letters!

This is the letter A.

It is the first letter of the alphabet. Look at the alphabet chart. Can you find A? It is at the beginning of the alphabet. Trace or write in the As on the ladder as you climb up to Amy's tree house.

Astronaut Andy has gone to the moon in search of As. Help him find all the As on the moon. Draw a circle around each A.

Hint: There are eight As.

Look, one is circled for you.

This is the letter B.

It is the second letter of the alphabet. Trace all the Bs on this page. Then write the letter B inside each empty balloon.

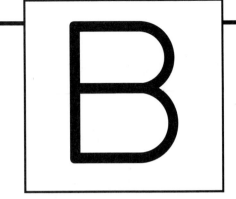

Let's take a trip to the zoo! As you walk along the path, look at the animals' names. Circle all the Bs you find.

Look, one is done for you.

Now look around the room you are in. Find three things with a B on them.

This is the letter C.

We're at the C museum, and you are the artist! Help to finish these works of art by tracing or writing in the letter C.

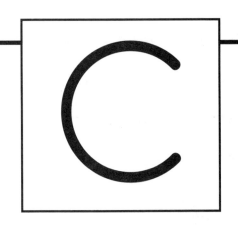

Christopher is thinking of something yummy to eat. Color all the shapes that have Cs in them to find out what it is. One shape is colored for you.

LET'S REVIEW

Let's review the letters we have learned so far. We have learned the first three letters of the alphabet. First trace them. Then write them yourself on the lines. Say each letter out loud as you write it.

_____   _____   _____

This is the letter D.

Look, it's snowing Ds! Trace the Ds in the snowflakes. Then write some of your own Ds inside the rest of the snowflakes.

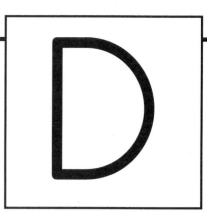

Here's some yummy Letter Cereal! Circle all the letter Ds. They are DELICIOUS!

Look, one is circled for you.

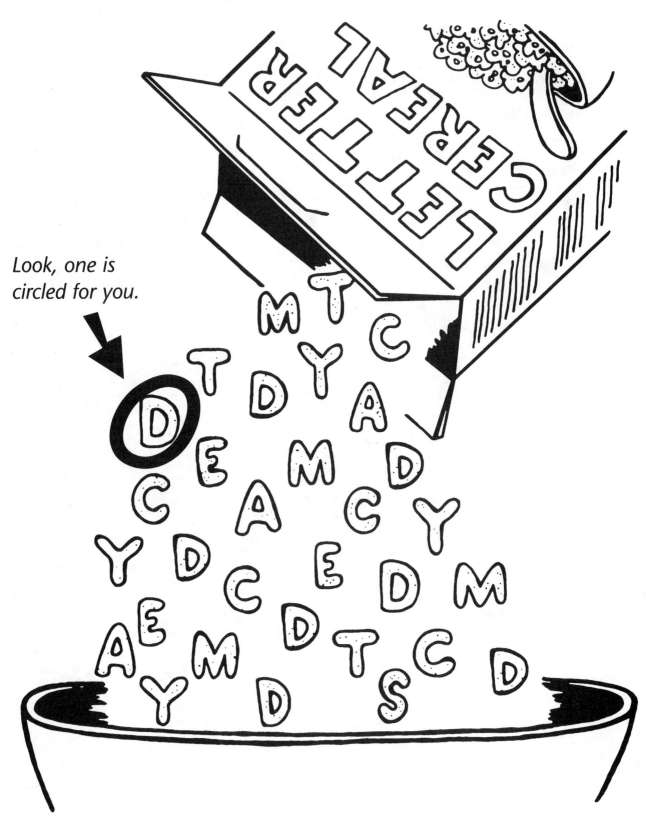

This is the letter E.

There are many places on this giant checkerboard for you to put the letter E. First trace all the Es you see. Then write an E in each empty space.

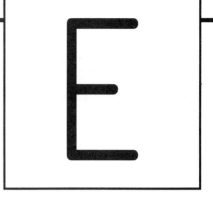

Here is a silly story about two friends, Kevin and Claire. Read it and put an X on all the letter Es you see.

Look, one is done for you.

LET'S REVIEW

This is a triangle: △. Write a D inside all the triangles.
This is a rectangle: ▯. Write an E inside all the rectangles.
Trace the letters that are already there.

LET'S REVIEW

These letters are all mixed up! Can you put them in the right order? Write them in the order of the alphabet on the blank lines.

B D A E C

___ ___ ___ ___ ___

When you are finished, you can use the alphabet chart to check your answers.

This is the letter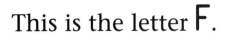

Play this game of hopscotch with Felicia. Fill in or trace the Fs as you hop along.

There are many Fs hiding under the circus big top. Can you find them all? Circle them.

Hint: There are six of them.

Look, one is circled for you.

Find three books in your home with an F on the cover.

This is the letter G.

It's raining Gs! Trace as many Gs as you can before they hit the ground. Then write your own Gs inside the raindrops.

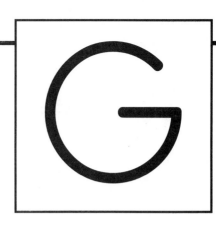

Find all the Gs in this letter ball. Color each shape that has a G in it. One shape is colored for you.

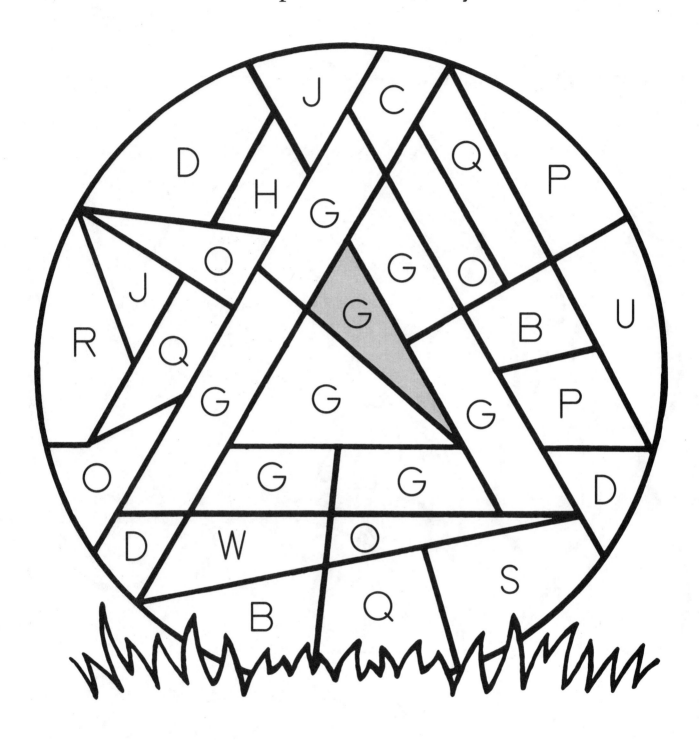

What shape did you make when you colored the shapes with Gs?

LET'S REVIEW

This page is filled with lots of fruits and vegetables. Use the chart below to help you color them with crayons.

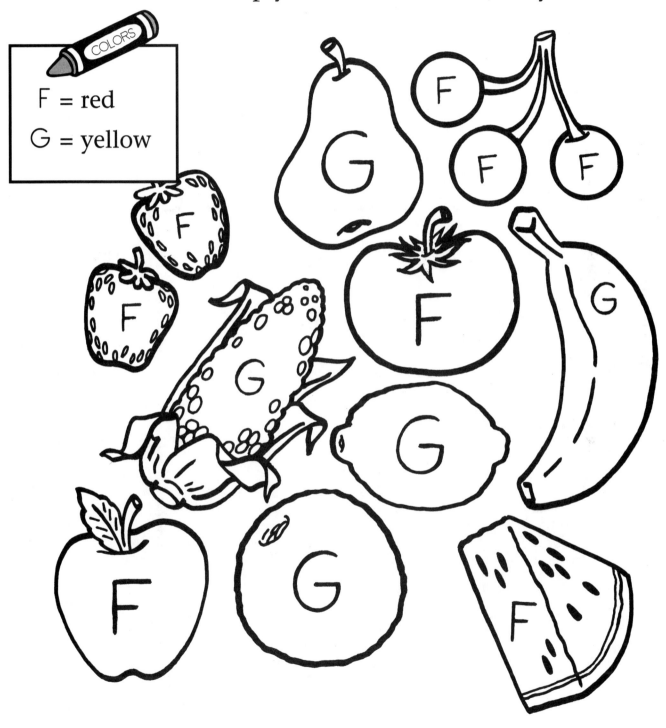

F = red
G = yellow

Can you name all these fruits and vegetables?

LET'S REVIEW

Here is a picture frame made of the letters D, E, F, and G. There is a different letter on each side of the frame. Fill in the missing letters. Then draw a picture of yourself inside the frame.

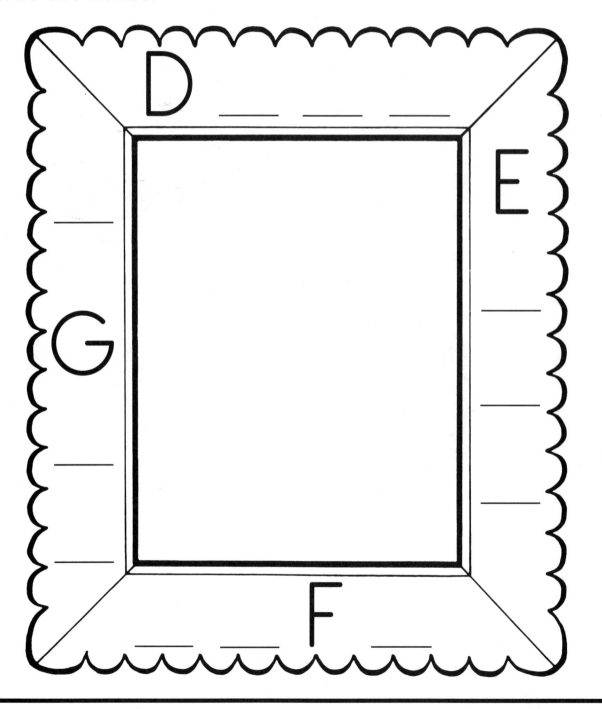

LET'S REVIEW

Use your pencil to connect the dots in order. Start with **A** and end with **G**.

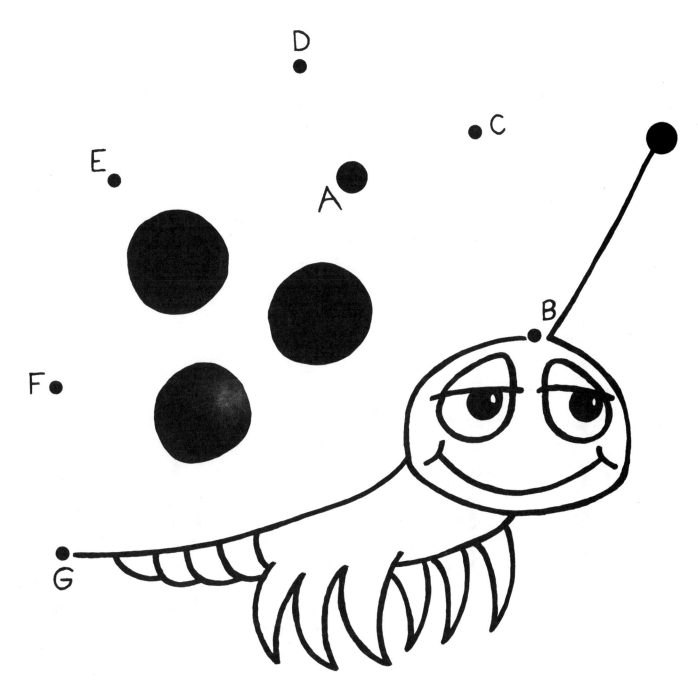

What did you make?

This is the letter H.

Hannah is climbing on the H jungle gym. Trace each H you see. Then write your own Hs on the blank lines.

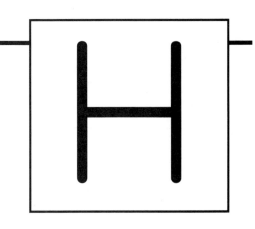

Can you find H on the alphabet chart? What letter comes before it? What letter comes after it?

Can you find all the Hs hiding in this playground? Circle each one.

Look, one is circled for you.

Hint: There are nine of them.

This is the letter I.

Isabel is blowing bubbles. Trace or write the letter I in all the big bubbles.

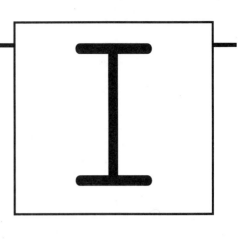

Find all the Is hidden at the beach and circle them.

Hint: There are nine of them.

Look, one is circled for you.

LET'S REVIEW

This is a circle O. Put an H in all the circles. This is a square □. Put an I in all the squares. Trace the letters that are already there.

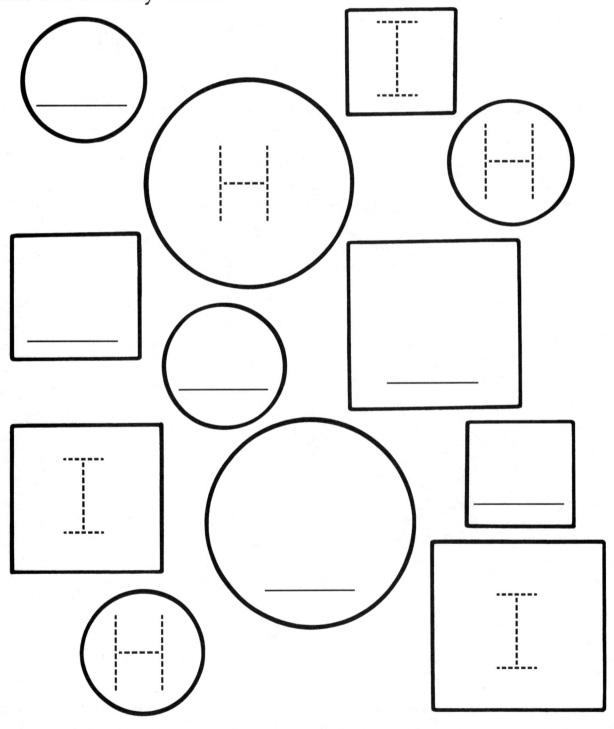

LET'S REVIEW

Beginning with A, draw a line from dot to dot until you get to I. Can you guess what the picture will be?

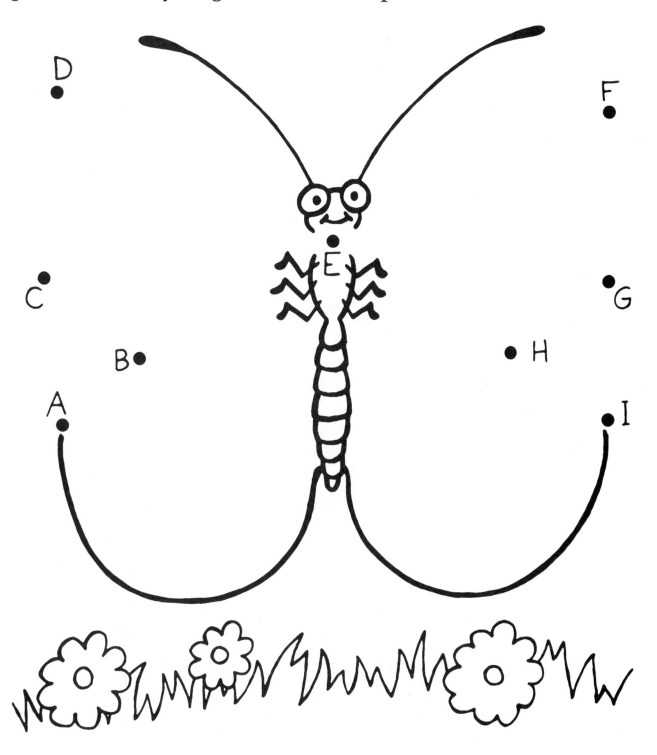

LET'S REVIEW

Now we have learned about the first nine letters of the alphabet. See if you can remember them. Write them in order on the lines below. Some letters have been filled in for you.

Start Here

___ ___ C

D ___ ___

___ H ___

End Here

"HURRAY!"

This is the letter J.

Here is the Jumping Js basketball team. Fill in or trace the Js on each person's shirt.

Help Jenna shop for Js. Circle all the Js you see.

Look, one has been circled for you.

Hint: There are eight of them.

Can you find two things in your refrigerator that have a J on them? What are they?

This is the letter K.

Kyle is building with blocks. Help him by tracing or writing the letter K on each block.

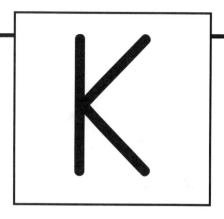

Color all the shapes that have **K**s in them and you will find two things you can play with. One shape has been colored for you.

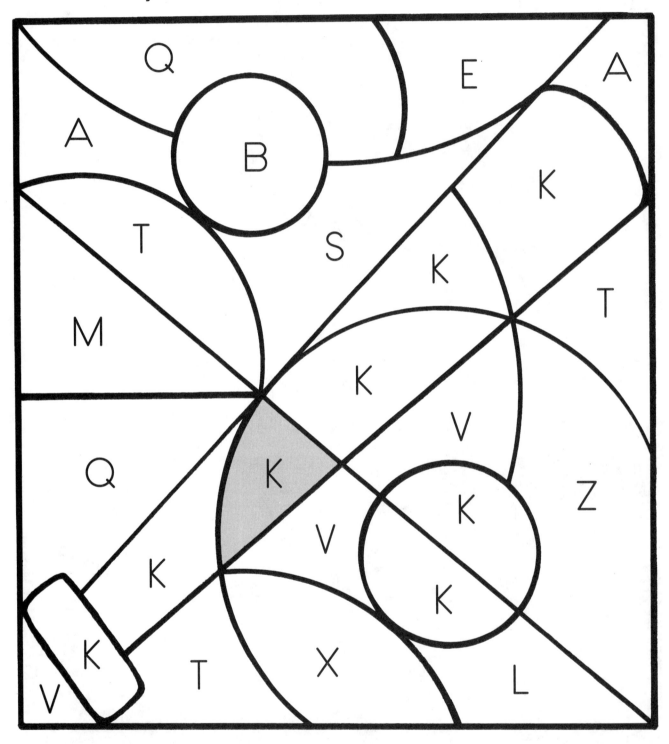

What can you do with these toys?

LET'S REVIEW

The class at Hill Street School is making flags with the letters **H, I, J,** and **K.** Trace the letters on the top row of flags. Then write the letters in the same order on the two rows of flags below.

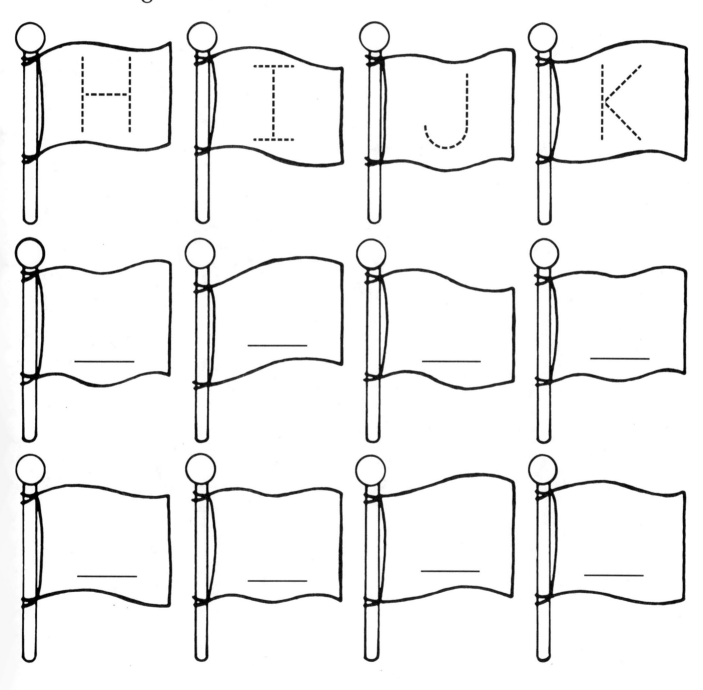

This is the letter L.

Lucas is picking giant L flowers for his mother. Trace each L that you see. Then write in any Ls that are missing.

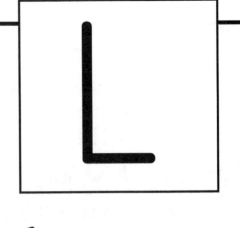

Lauren is going on a scuba diving hunt for Ls. Help her find all the Ls in the ocean. Circle each one.

Hint: There are seven of them.

Look, one is circled for you.

Sing the alphabet song up to the letter L. What letter will come next?

LET'S REVIEW

Jessica is flying her letter kite. It is so long, it goes over to the next page! Use the color chart on the next page to help make Jessica's kite colorful.

40

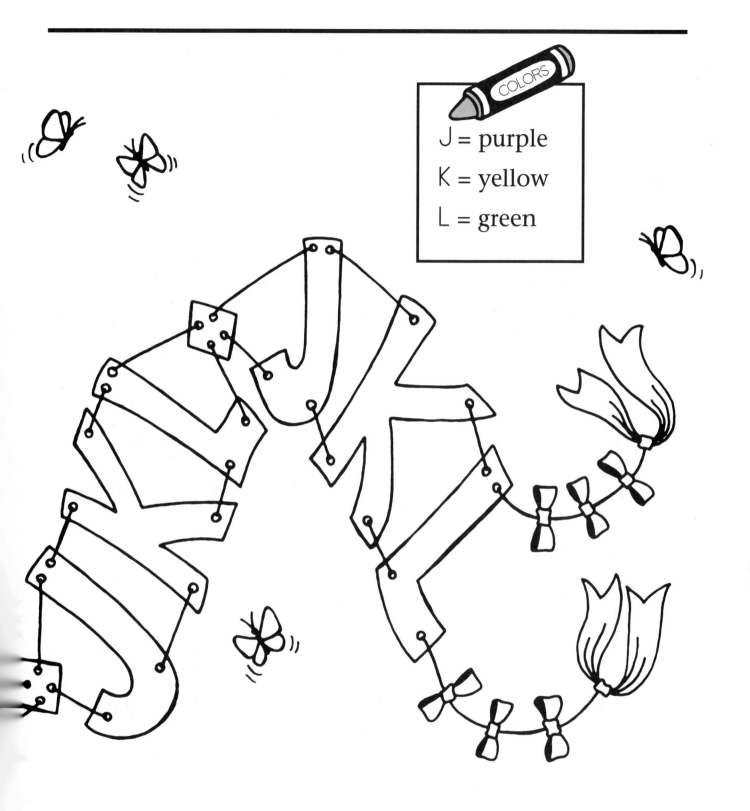

LET'S REVIEW

Here's a silly alphabet clock! Fill in the letters from A to L as you go around the clock. Look at the alphabet chart if you need help.

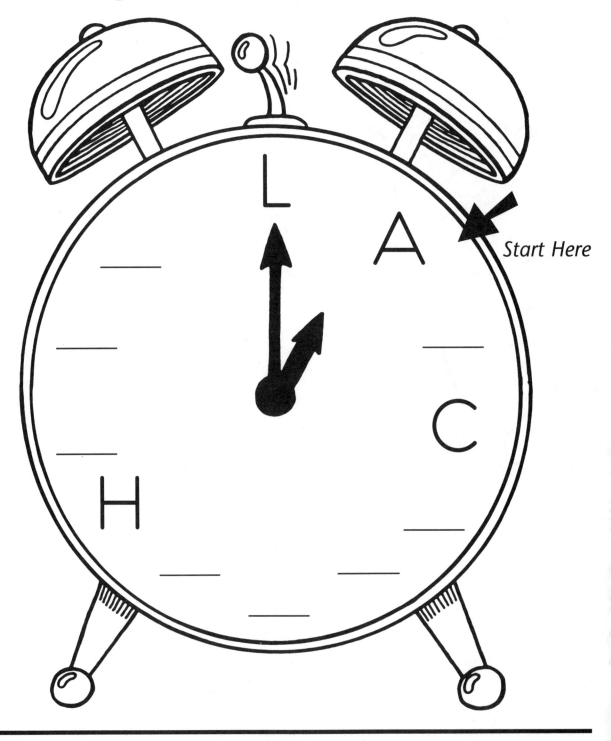

This is the letter M.

Let's take a ride on the M train with engineer Mike. Trace or write the letter M inside the boxcars.

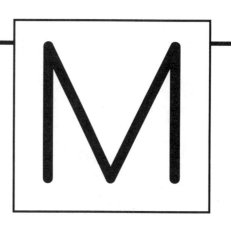

It's a windy day, and all of Michelle's letters have blown out of her box. M is her favorite letter. Find and circle all the Ms you see.

Look, one has been circled for you.

This is the letter N.

Nicole is wearing letter jewelry. Trace or write all the missing Ns on her necklace, earrings, and bracelet.

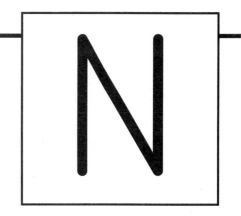

Let's take a trip to the ice-cream store! Look at the list of flavors. Circle all the **N**s. One **N** has been circled for you.

Now find as many **N**s as you can on the boxes and cans in your kitchen cupboard.

LET'S REVIEW

This page is filled with many letters. Put an **X** on all the **M**s. Circle all the **N**s.

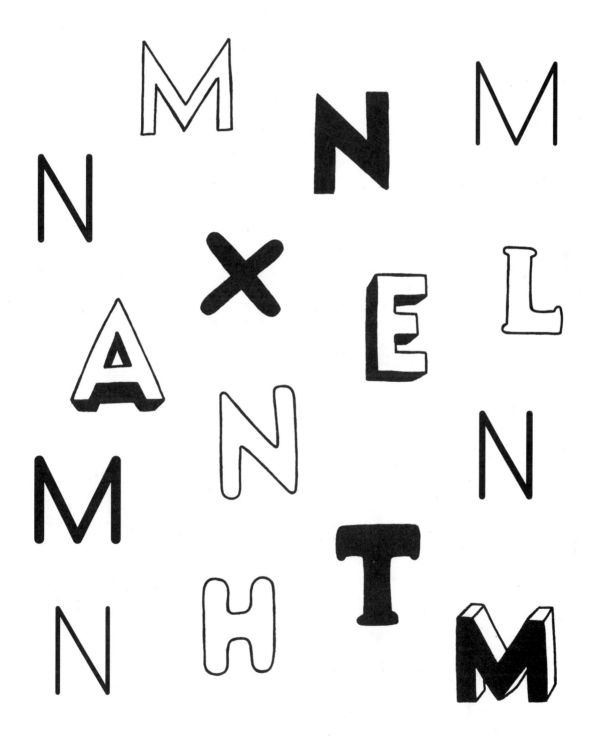

LET'S REVIEW

WOW! Here's a letter snake! Fill in the missing letters. Make sure the letters are in the right order. Look at your alphabet chart if you need help.

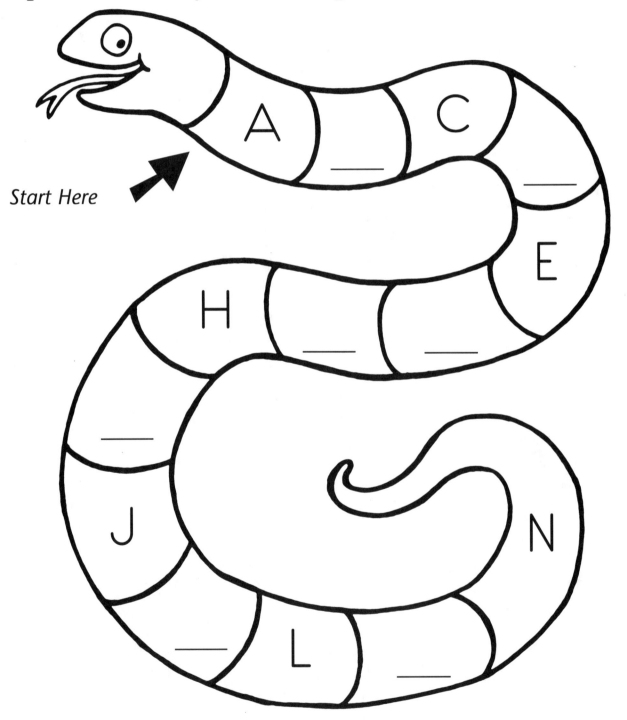

Start Here

This is the letter O.

Os are growing on this tree! Trace all the Os on the tree. Then write in more Os on the blank lines.

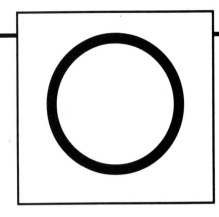

Color all the shapes that have Os in them to find something that lives in the ocean. One shape has been colored for you.

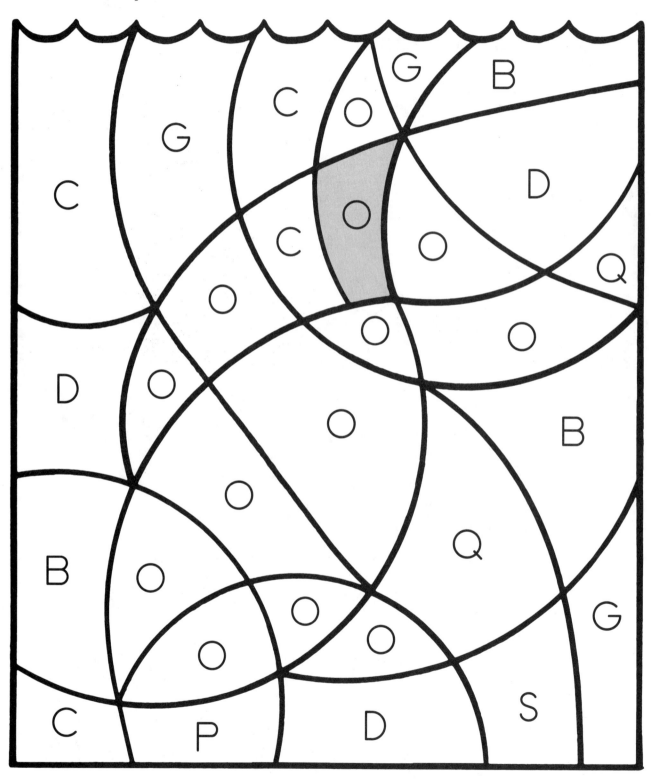

This is the letter P.

Trace or fill in the Ps as you go along the path.

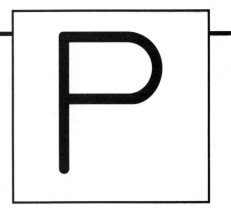

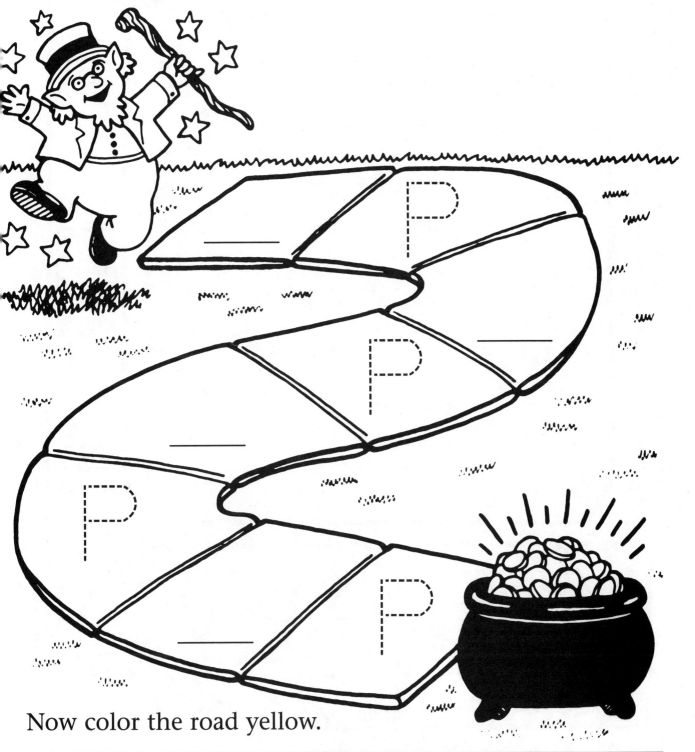

Now color the road yellow.

Let's watch this special TV show. It's all about the alphabet. Can you find all the Ps? Draw a circle around each one.

Look, one has been circled for you.

LET'S REVIEW

Here's some yummy alphabet soup! Sam only likes to eat Os and Ps. Put an X on all the Os and circle all the Ps so Sam can find them. A few are done for you.

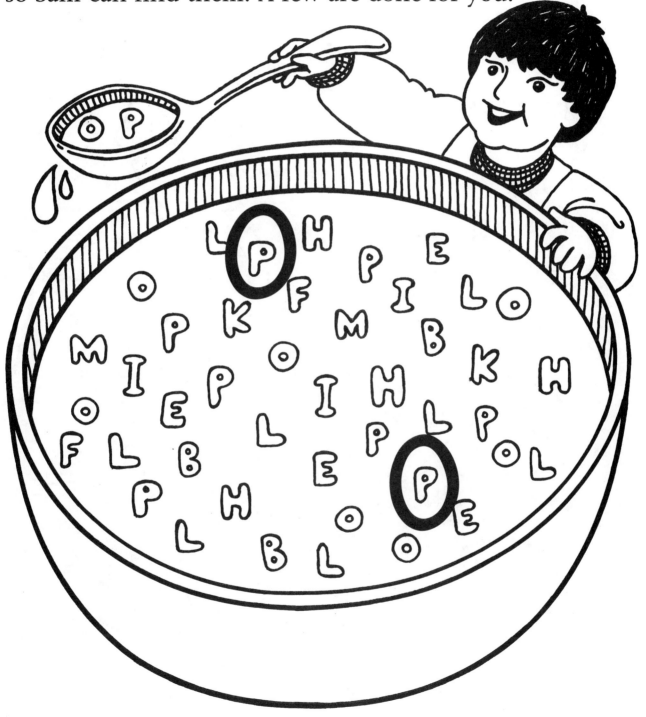

LET'S REVIEW

Let's review the last five letters we have learned—L, M, N, O, and P. Look at the color chart. Then color this silly monster.

L = green
M = yellow
N = orange
O = blue
P = black

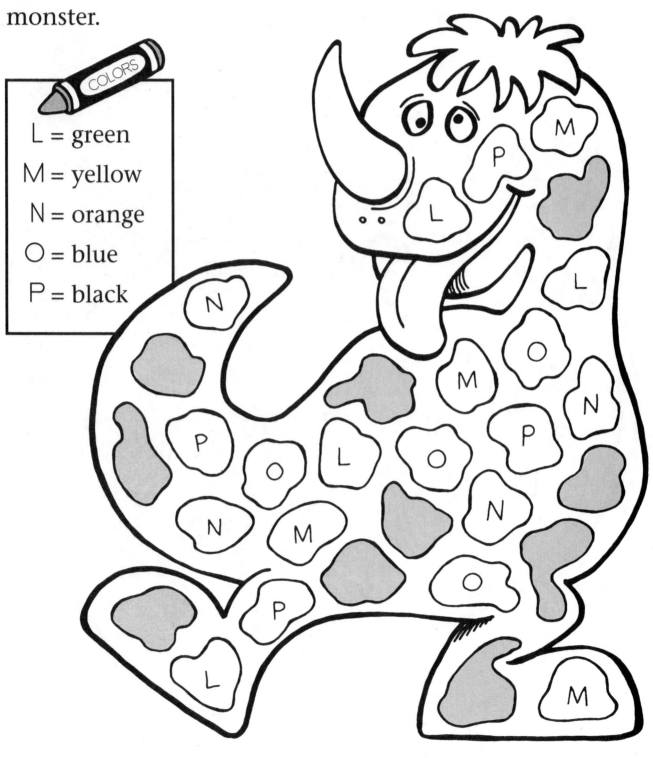

LET'S REVIEW

These letters are all mixed up! Can you put them in the right order? Write them in the order of the alphabet on the blank lines.

P M L O N

___ ___ ___ ___ ___

When you are finished, use the alphabet chart to check your answers.

This is the letter Q.

Here is a book filled with Q words. Help complete the pages below by tracing or writing in all the missing Qs.

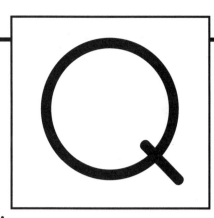

QUACK

QUAKE

QUEEN

QUAINT

____UICK

____UIET

____UILT

____UOTES

Welcome to Letter Land, where letters are growing everywhere you look. Watch out—a letter might pop up right under you! Draw an ✗ on all the Qs you see.

Look, one has been done for you.

This is the letter R.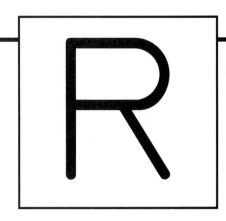

Help complete this crossword puzzle by tracing or writing Rs in all the squares that need them.

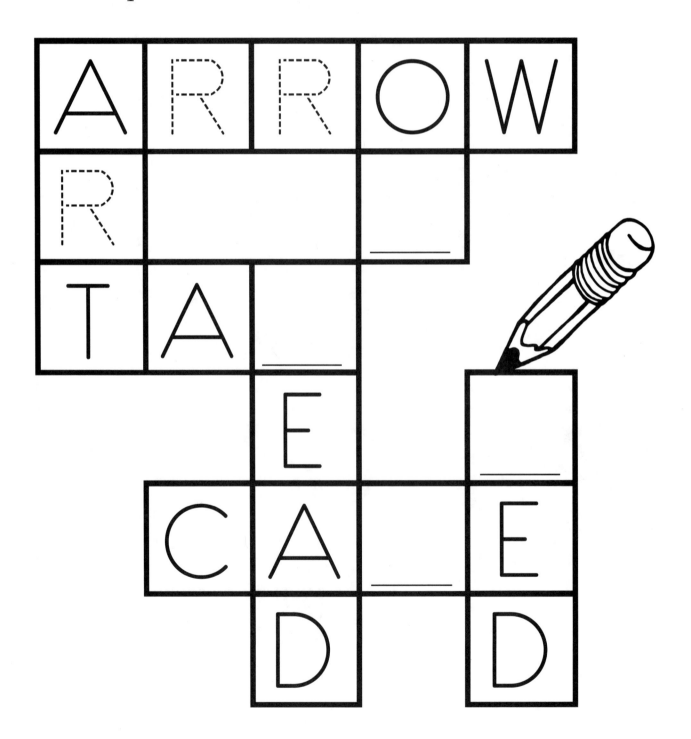

This special tree grows letter leaves! Put an ✗ on all the leaves that have Rs on them. One is done for you.

Now see if you can find three toys or games around your home that have an R on them.

This is the letter S.

Susie and Steven are at the library. Help them organize the books by tracing or writing the letter S on all the books that are missing titles.

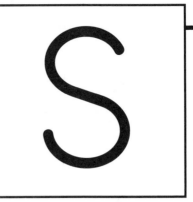

Color all the shapes that have an S in them to find something you can see in the sky. One shape is colored for you.

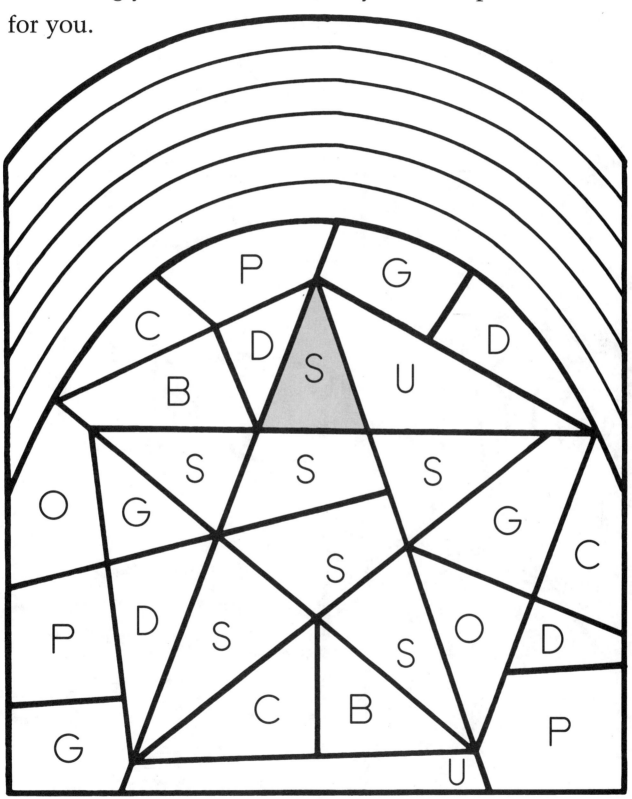

When you are finished, color the rainbow.

LET'S REVIEW

Casey is stringing together beads with the letters Q, R, and S. Trace the letters, then help him fill in the rest of the letters. Be sure to follow the pattern that he started.

Start Here

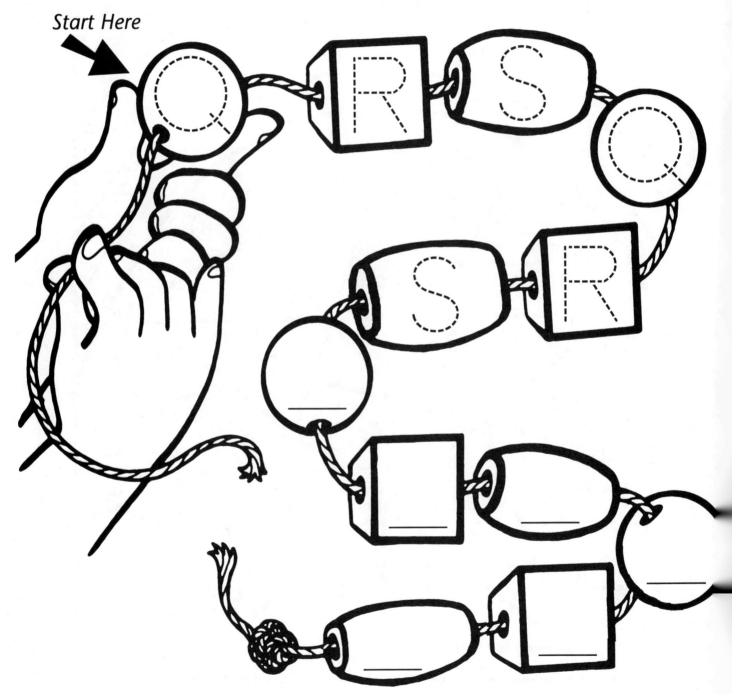

This is the letter T.

We're in the T galaxy. Trace or write Ts inside all these outer-space objects.

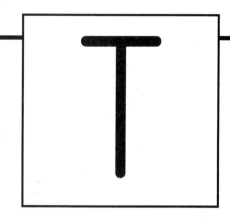

Terry is spinning the letter wheel to win a prize. If it stops on the letter T, he will win. Help Terry by circling all the Ts on the wheel. One T has been circled for you.

LET'S REVIEW

Welcome to the Letter Hall of Fame. This trophy case holds all the letters we have learned so far—from A to T. But some letters are missing. Write them on the lines.

When you are done, use the alphabet chart to see if you wrote all the letters correctly.

This is the letter U.

Ursula is putting together a jigsaw puzzle of the letter U. Help her finish the puzzle by tracing or writing a U on each puzzle piece.

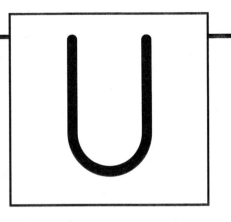

Umm! Look at all the yummy things to eat at the U bakery. Color the goodies that have Us on them. One has been colored for you.

This is the letter V.

This creature loves to eat rock cookies that have Vs on them. Trace or write a V on each one of his cookies.

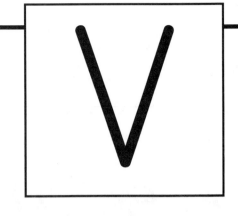

There are many Vs hiding in this toy store. Find and circle them.

Hint: There are seven Vs.

Look, one has been circled for you.

LET'S REVIEW

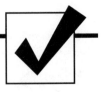

These are the T, U, and V stairs. Trace the letters on the bottom step. Then follow the pattern and fill in the letters on the other two steps.

Hint: The letters are in the order of the alphabet.

LET'S REVIEW

Here is a rainbow made of the letters Q, R, S, T, U, and V! Find each of these letters on the alphabet chart. Say each one out loud. Then use the color chart below to color in the rainbow.

Q = red
R = blue
S = green
T = yellow
U = orange
V = violet

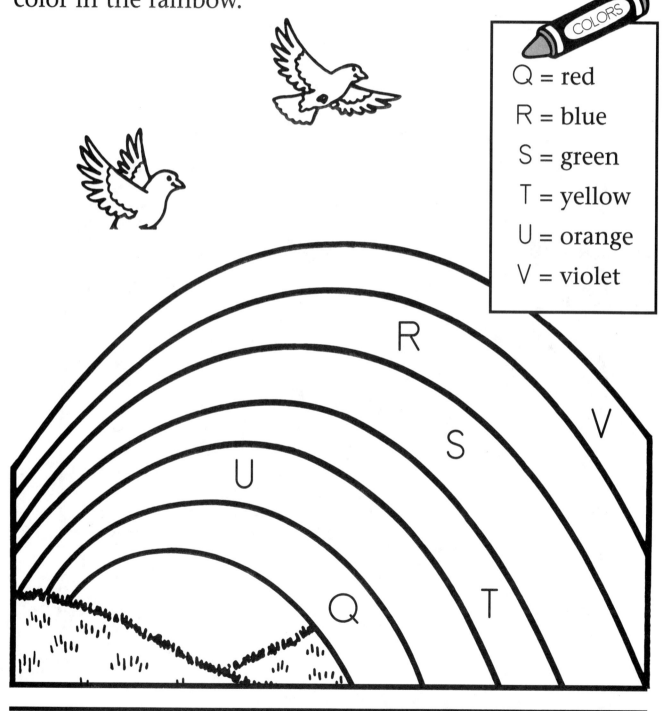

This is the letter W.

The kids are learning to paint Ws in art class today. Help them finish all the paintings by tracing or writing in the Ws.

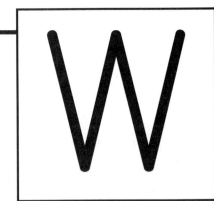

William is playing the letter song. Find all of the Ws coming out of his saxophone and circle them.

Look, one is circled for you.

LET'S REVIEW

Here's another silly alphabet clock. This clock starts with the letter L. Fill in the letters as you go around the clock. Look at the alphabet chart if you need help.

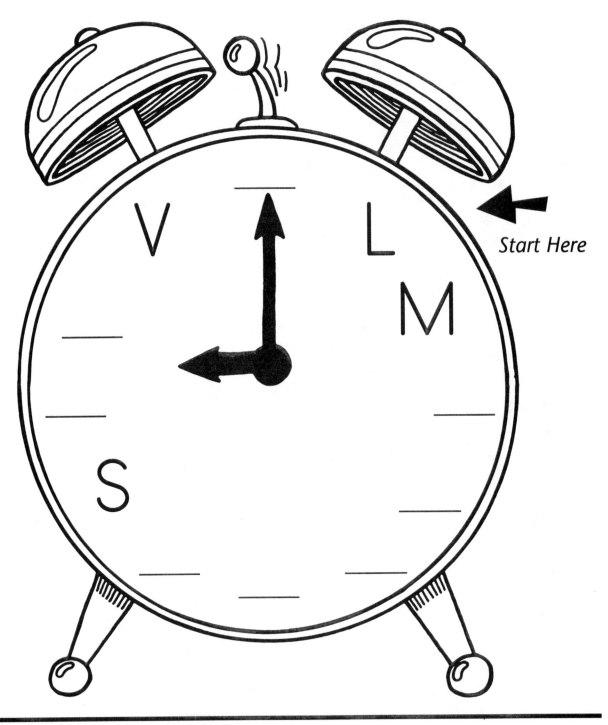

Start Here

This is the letter X.

Take a trip to the top of the X skyscraper. Trace or write in the missing Xs on the windows as you go up.

Color all the shapes that have Xs in them to see what's growing inside the letter vase. One shape has been colored for you.

LET'S REVIEW

This clown is juggling letters! Put Ws in the circles and Xs in the squares. Trace the letters that are already there.

This is the letter Y.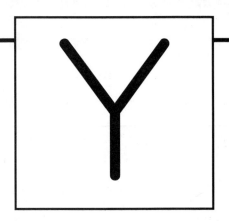

Dylan wants to fill his entire computer screen with Ys. You can help him. Trace or write in the Ys on the computer screen.

Yolanda's favorite thing to drink is Y juice. She is buying every can of Y juice in the vending machine. Help her find all the cans of Y juice by circling them.

Look, one is circled for you.

This is the letter Z.

Zoë is snoring in her sleep. Trace or write in all the Zs coming out of her mouth.

We're on a safari searching for Zs. Let's find all the Zs in the jungle and circle them.

Hint: There are eight of them.

Look, one is circled for you.

LET'S REVIEW

Here's a letter pyramid! Color all the Ys yellow and all the Zs green.

LET'S REVIEW

These letters are all mixed up! Can you put them in the correct order? Write them in the order of the alphabet on the blank lines.

Y X Z W

___ ___ ___ ___

When you are finished, use the alphabet chart to check your answers.

LET'S REVIEW

Use the color chart below to color this superhero.

W = brown
X = blue
Y = red
Z = yellow

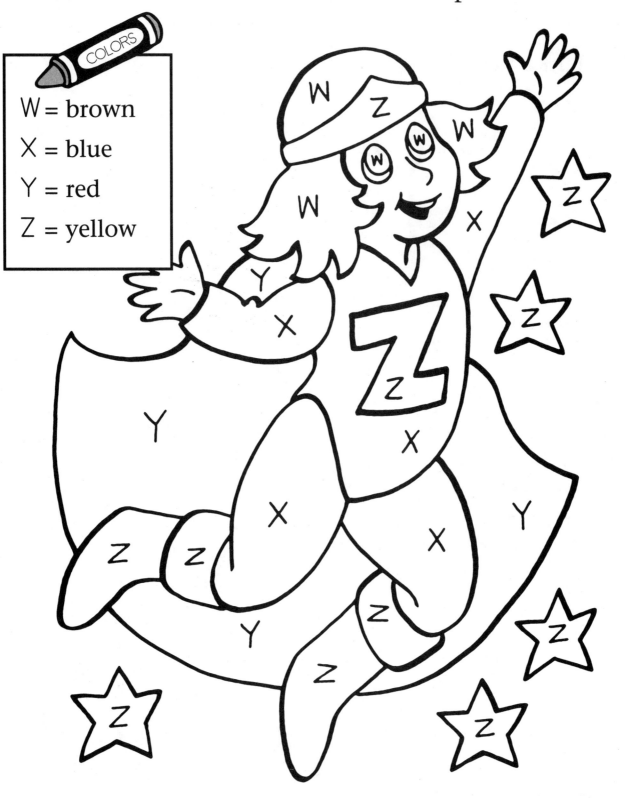

LET'S REVIEW

Here's another letter snake. This snake begins at L and goes all the way to Z. Fill in the missing letters. Make sure the letters are in the right order.

Start Here

When you are finished, use the alphabet chart to check your answers.

LET'S REVIEW

We have learned all the letters of the alphabet from A to Z. Let's see how much you can remember. Begin with the letter A and draw from dot to dot until you reach the letter Z. What picture have you created? There are more dot-to-dots on the next few pages.

LET'S REVIEW

Begin with the letter A and draw from dot to dot until you reach the letter Z. What picture have you made?

What uppercase letters are on your tube of toothpaste?

LET'S REVIEW

Begin with the letter A and draw from dot to dot until you reach the letter Z. What animal have you created?

LET'S REVIEW

Begin with the letter A and draw from dot to dot until you reach the letter Z. What picture have you created?

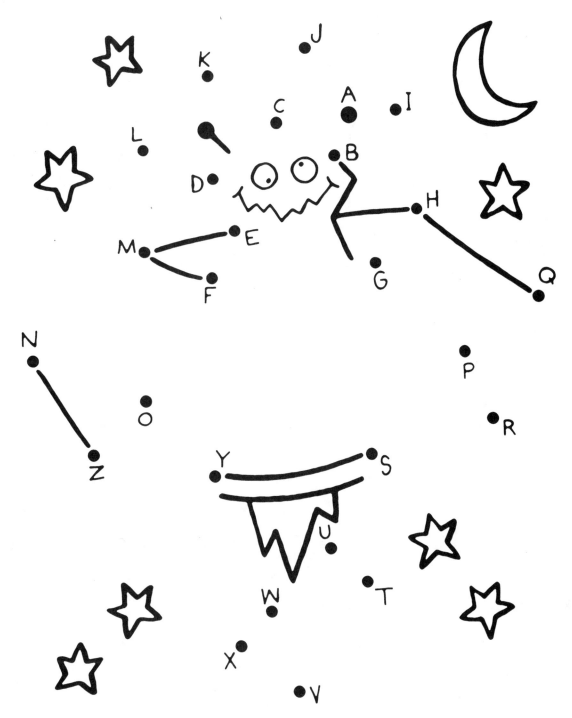

What uppercase letters are on your pencil or crayon?

LET'S REVIEW

Fill in the letter that comes next in each row. Use the alphabet chart to check your answers.

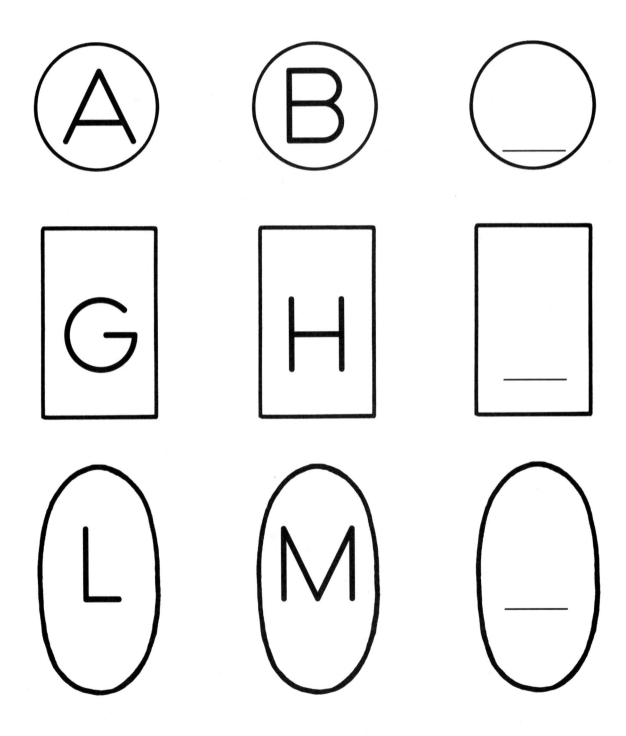

LET'S REVIEW

Fill in the letter that comes next in each row. Use the alphabet chart to check your answers.

LET'S REVIEW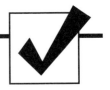

Fill in the letter that comes next in each row. Use the alphabet chart to check your answers.

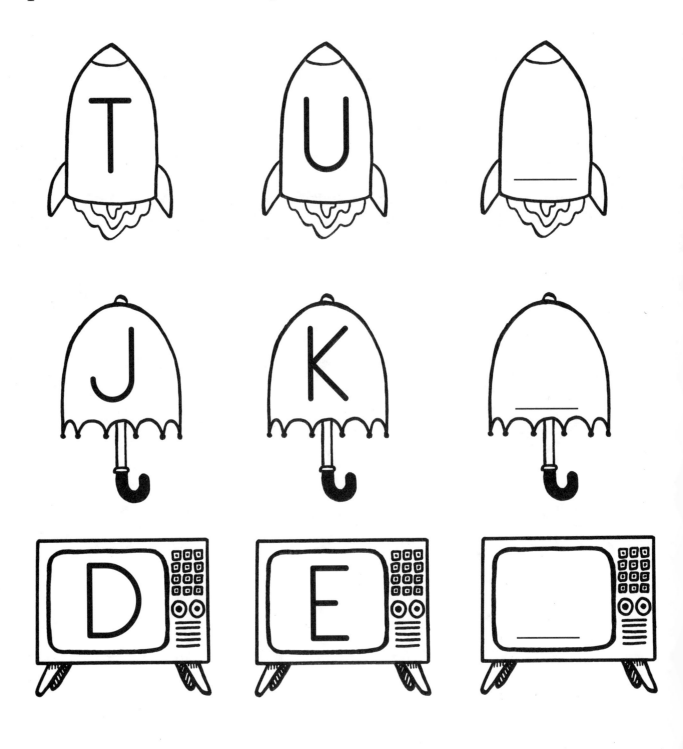

LET'S REVIEW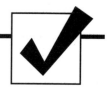

Fill in the letter that comes first in each row. Use the alphabet chart to check your answers.

LET'S REVIEW

Fill in the letter that comes first in each row. Use the alphabet chart to check your answers.

LET'S REVIEW

Fill in the letter that comes first in each row. Use the alphabet chart to check your answers.

KID'S NOTE

Now that you've learned all about uppercase letters, it's time to learn the lowercase letters. Use the alphabet chart at the back of this book. Are you ready? Grab a crayon or pencil, and let's go!

This is the letter a.

It is the first letter of the alphabet. Look at the alphabet chart. Can you find a? Where is it? That's right, it is at the beginning of the alphabet.

Billy Bunny is hopping from a to a. Trace or write in the as for him to hop on.

Now there are many different letters for Billy Bunny to hop on. Circle all the **a**s.

*Look, one **a** has been circled for you.*

This is the letter **b**.

Trace or write the letter **b** inside the petals and the center of this sunflower.

Color the shapes with **b**s inside them to find something we all have inside us. One shape is colored for you.

Find as many **b**s as you can on the back of a cereal box in your kitchen cupboard.

This is the letter **c**.

Christopher and Christina are playing the Letter Game. Trace or write the letter **c** on the empty squares of the game board.

Erica likes to catch letters with her special letter catcher. Today, she is catching **c**s. Put an X on all the **c**s you see. *Look, one X has been drawn for you.*

LET'S REVIEW

Let's review the letters we have learned so far. We have learned the first three letters of the alphabet. First trace them. Then write them yourself on the lines. Say each letter out loud as you write it.

a   b   c

___   ___   ___

This is the letter d.

Andrea is shopping at the hat store. Here are all the d hats. Trace or write the letter d on each hat.

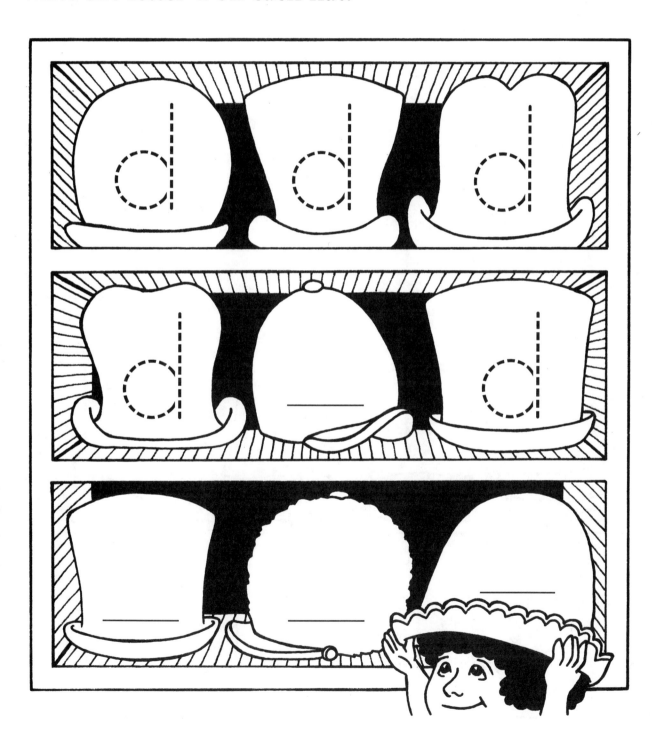

Look at the many different letter hats Andrea has to choose from. Circle the hats with **d**s on them.

Look, one **d** *has been circled for you.*

This is the letter **e**.

Let's take a trip to the pyramids in ancient Egypt. Trace or write an **e** on all the pyramids you see.

What shape are these pyramids?

These pyramids have many different letters on them. Put an X on each pyramid that has an **e** on it.

Look, one X has been drawn for you.

LET'S REVIEW

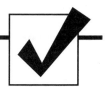

This is a triangle: △. Write a **d** inside all the triangles. This is a rectangle: ▭. Write an **e** inside all the rectangles. Trace the letters that are already there.

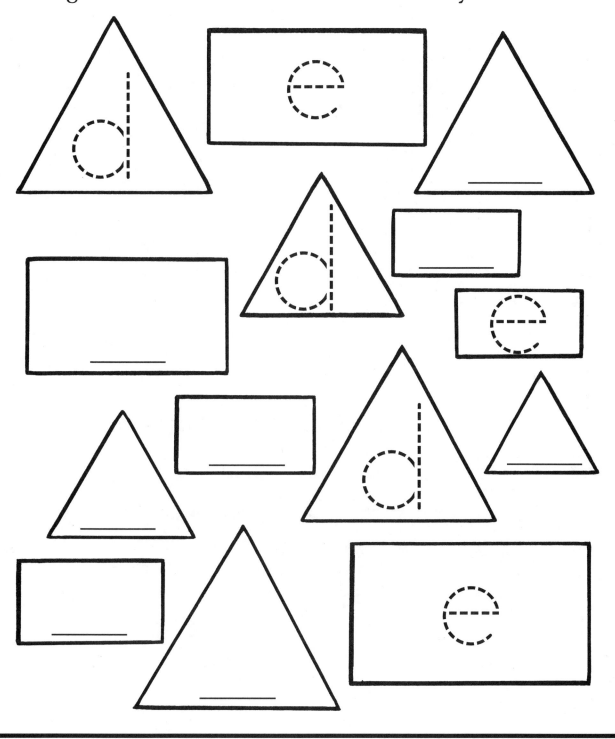

LET'S REVIEW

These letters are all mixed up! Can you put them in the right order? Write them in the order of the alphabet on the blank lines.

b d a e c

___ ___ ___ ___ ___

When you are finished, you can use the alphabet chart to check your answers.

This is the letter f.

Chelsea the chicken has laid some eggs. Trace or write an f on all the eggs you see.

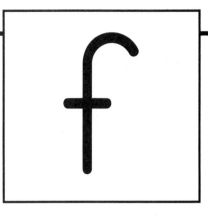

Now Chelsea the chicken's eggs are in a carton. They are ready to go to the store. Put an X on each egg with an f on it.

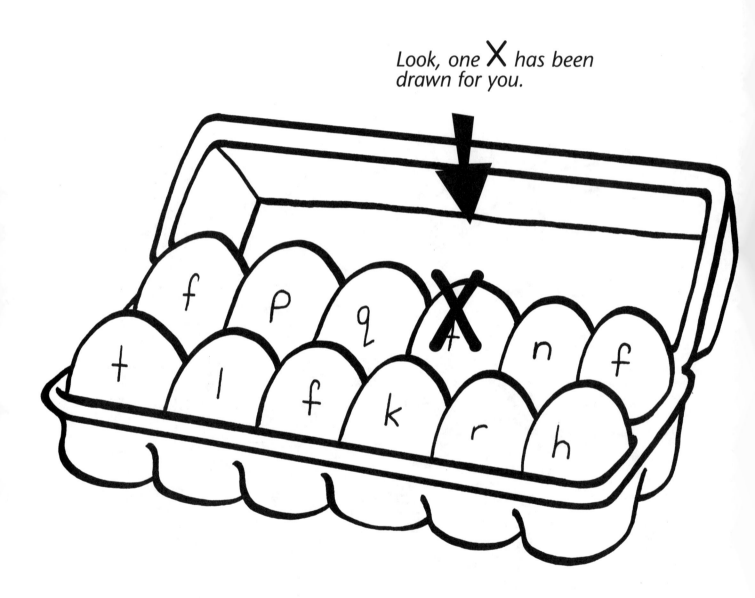

Look, one X has been drawn for you.

Now open your favorite book and find a page with at least four fs on it.

This is the letter g.

Welcome to the g galaxy. Trace all the gs you see. Then write gs on the rest of the objects in the galaxy.

We have now entered the alphabet galaxy, where the stars and planets have many different letters on them. Put an X on all the planets and stars that have gs on them.
Look, one X has been drawn for you.

LET'S REVIEW

Look at this funny monster. Use the color chart below to help you color his spots.

f = yellow
g = green

Now color the rest of the monster any way you like.

LET'S REVIEW

Say the letters on these clowns' tummies out loud. Then trace or write the letter shown on each clown's tummy inside the balloons that clown is holding.

LET'S REVIEW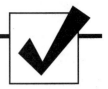

Use your favorite color crayon to connect the dots in order. Start with **a** and end with **g**.

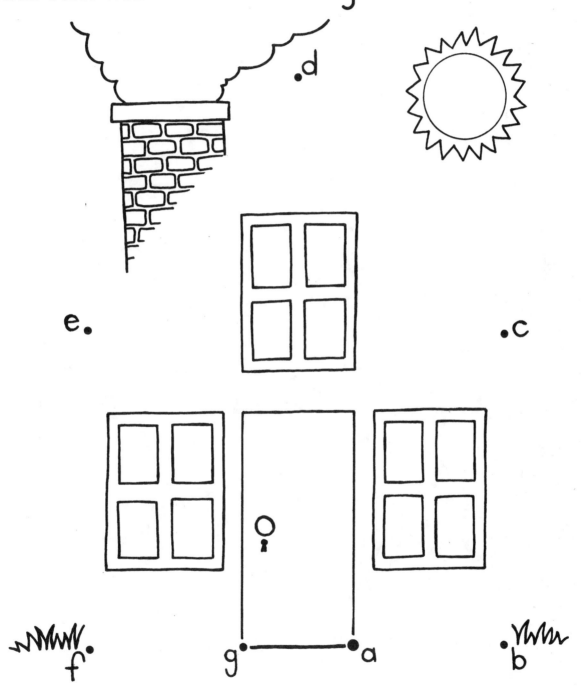

What did you make?

This is the letter h.

This happy monster loves hs. Trace the hs in the monster's antennae and nose. Then write hs on his hands and feet.

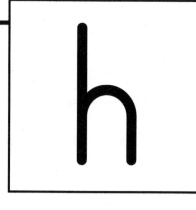

There are many letters on this bashful monster. Put an X on all the hs you see.

Look, one X has been drawn for you.

This is the letter **i**.

Help Traci complete the crossword puzzle below. Trace all the letter **i**s you see. Then write **i**s inside the empty boxes.

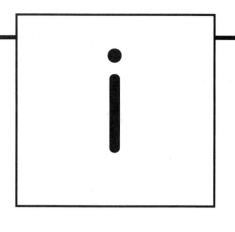

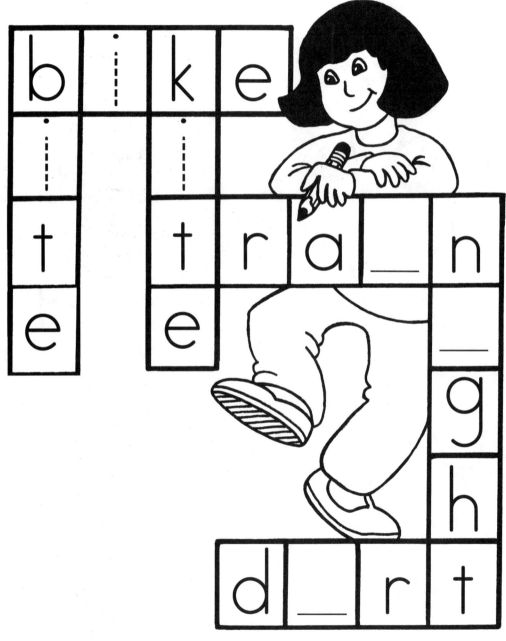

How many words did you make?

Detective Dennis is searching for clues to solve the mystery of the hidden **i**s. Help him by circling all the **i**s you find.

Hint: There are eight of them.   Look, one **i** has been circled for you.

LET'S REVIEW

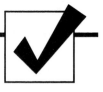

This is a circle: O. Put the letter **h** inside all the circles. This is a square: □. Put an **i** inside all the squares. Trace the letters that are already there.

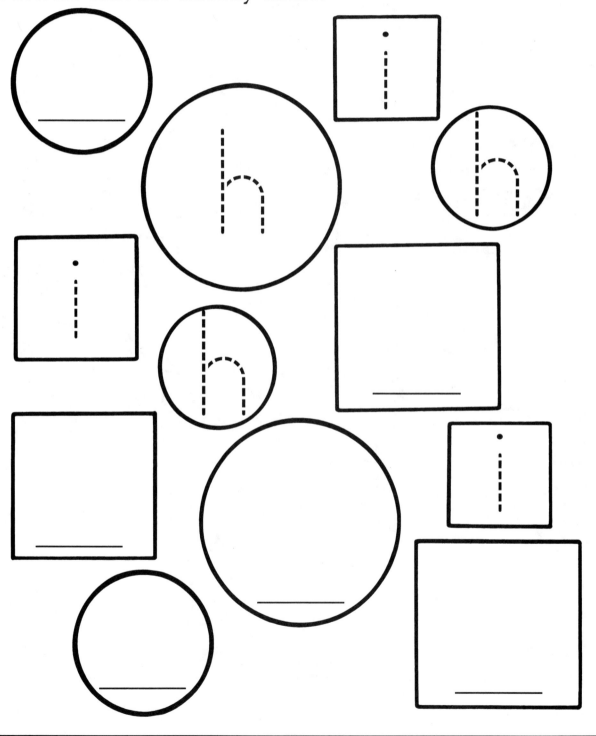

LET'S REVIEW

Use your pencil to connect the dots in order. Start with **a** and end with **i**. Can you guess what the picture will be?

LET'S REVIEW

Now we have learned about the first nine letters of the alphabet. See if you can remember them. Write or trace the letters on the lines below.

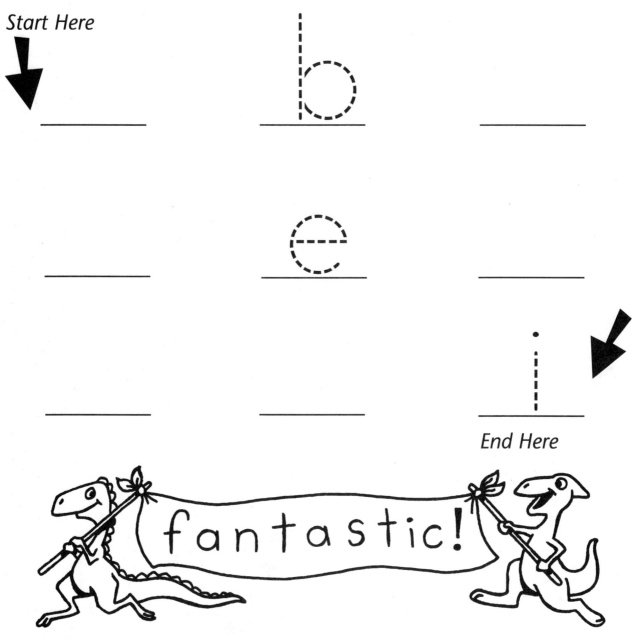

When you are finished, you can use the alphabet chart to check your answers.

This is the letter j.

Benjamin is stacking boxes of different sizes in his garage. Trace or write the letter j on each box.

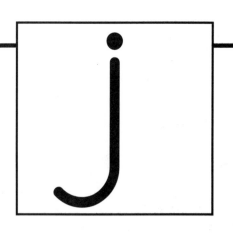

Color all the shapes that have js in them to see what's wrapped inside this gift box. One is colored for you.

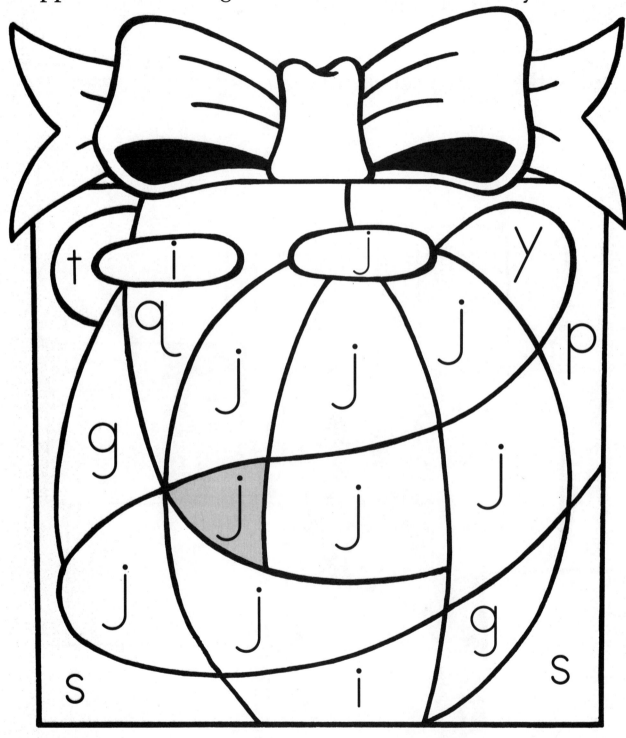

Now find five js on things you use in the bathroom, like shampoo or toothpaste.

This is the letter k.

The letter k school bus is on its way to the letter k school. Trace or write k inside each window of the bus.

Today, Erica is catching **k**s. Circle all the **k**s you see.
*Look, one **k** has been circled for you.*

LET'S REVIEW

Nicole is stacking **h, i, j,** and **k** blocks. Trace the letters in each pile. Then fill in the rest of the blocks in each pile with the correct letter.

This is the letter l.

There are many l clouds floating in the sky today.
Trace or write an l on each cloud.

Color all the shapes with **l**s to find something that brings us light and keeps us warm. One shape has been colored for you.

Now sing the alphabet song up to the letter **l**. What letter will come next?

LET'S REVIEW

Follow the footprints to the next page to see where they lead. Trace the letters j, k, and l on the first few footprints. Then write the letters in the same order on the rest of the footprints.

Start Here

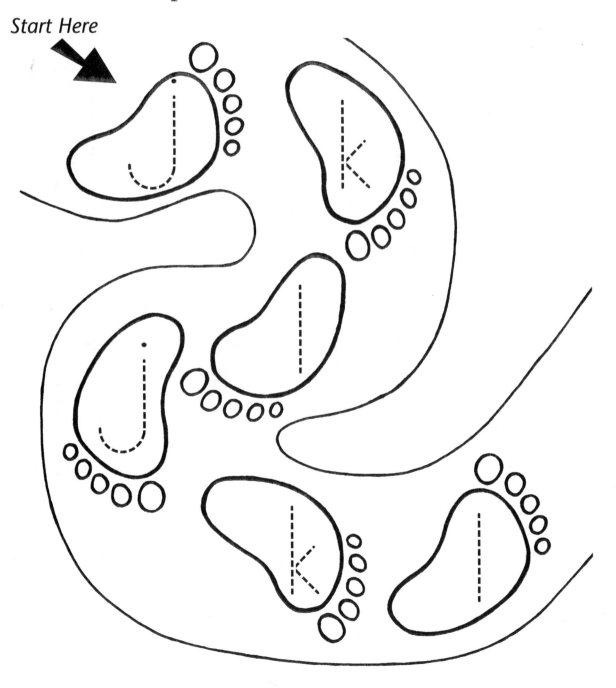

End Here

LET'S REVIEW

Katie is using her letter ruler to measure how tall Heather is. Write the letters **a** through **l** in order on the ruler. Start at the bottom of the ladder and write the letters in order up to the top.

Hint: Look at your alphabet chart if you need help.

What letter shows how tall Heather is?

This is the letter **m**.

Look at the many different shapes on this page. Trace or write the letter **m** inside each shape.

Eric is putting letter marbles into his giant jar. Draw an X on all the marbles that have the letter m on them.

Look, one X has been drawn for you.

What letter does the word **marble** begin with?

This is the letter n.

Sarah's grandmother is making a letter quilt for Sarah's bed. Trace or write the letter n inside each empty square.

This letter quilt has many different letters. Circle all the ns you see. *Look, one n has been circled for you.*

Find five ns on any of your toys or games.

LET'S REVIEW

This page is filled with many letters. Put an X on all the ms and circle all the ns.

Look, an X and a circle have been drawn for you.

LET'S REVIEW

Wow! Here's a letter caterpillar! Fill in the missing letters. Make sure the letters from a to n are in the correct order. Look at your alphabet chart if you need help.

Start Here

This is the letter o.

Take a ride on the letter Ferris wheel! Trace or write an o on all the seats.

This giant Ferris wheel has lots of different letters on it. Put an X on all the os you see.

Look, one X has been drawn for you.

This is the letter **p**.

Trace or write a **p** inside each ice-cream cone. Then color the cones your favorite flavors.

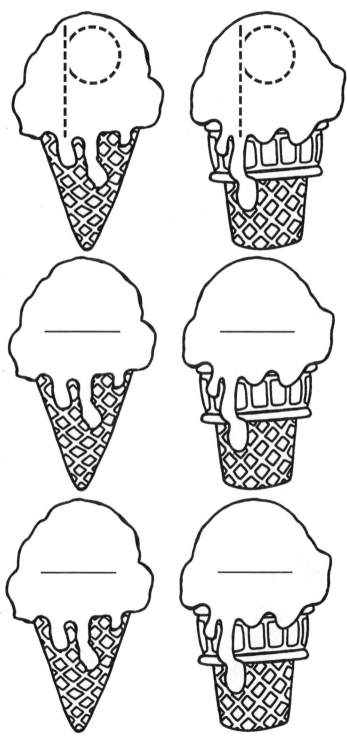

Look around the classroom and find the hidden **p**s. Circle each p you find.

Hint: There are eight of them.   Look, one p has been circled for you.

LET'S REVIEW

Color the shapes that have **o**s or **p**s in them to see two things you can find in the sky. Two shapes have been colored for you.

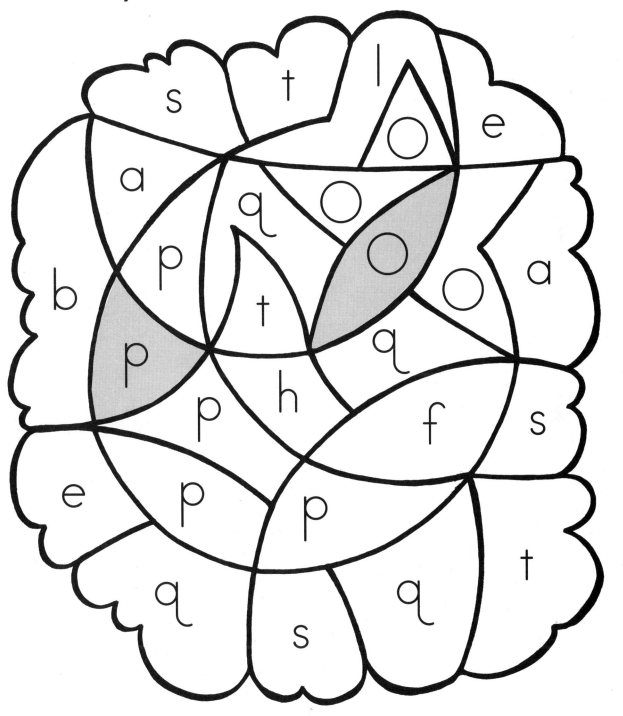

LET'S REVIEW

These letters are all mixed up! Can you put them in the correct order? Write them on the blank lines.

p m l o n

_ _ _ _ _

When you are finished, you can use the alphabet chart to check your answers.

This is the letter q.

Follow the bouncing balls down the page. Trace or write the letter q inside each ball as you go along.

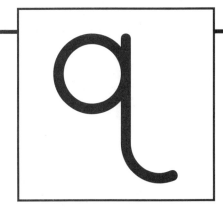

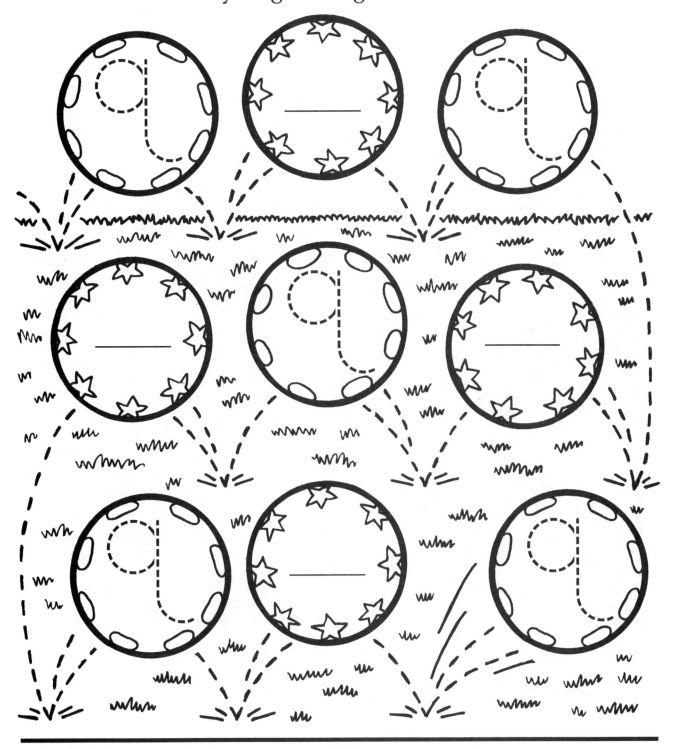

Find all the q s that are hidden at the amusement park. Circle each q you find.

Hint: There are nine of them.   *Look, one q has been circled for you.*

This is the letter **r**.

Erin is making letter pizza! Yum! Trace or write an **r** on each pepperoni slice.

Darren also loves to make letter pizza. He has put many different letters on top of his pizza. Put an X on all the rs you see.

Look, one X has been drawn for you.

This is the letter **s**.

Susana loves lollipops! Help her label each lollipop below with the letter **s**. Trace or write an **s** on each lollipop. Then color them your favorite flavor!

S

Nelson is mailing a letter to his friend Cassandra. Put an X on each **s** you see on the envelope.

Look, one X has been drawn for you.

LET'S REVIEW

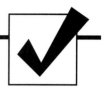

Use the color chart below to color this clown.

This is the letter t.

You can make many words by tracing or writing ts in this crossword puzzle.

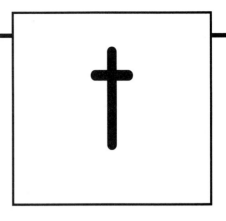

Kathy's bedroom is a mess! Help her find all the **t**s hiding in her room. Circle each one you find.

Hint: There are eight of them.

Look, one **t** has been circled for you.

155

LET'S REVIEW

Some of these letter fish have lost their letters. Write the letters that are missing from **a** to **t** on the fish. Make sure you write the letters in the correct order of the alphabet. Look at your alphabet chart if you need help.

This is the letter **u**.

Jennifer is watering her letter garden. Trace or write the letter **u** on all her carrots.

What color are carrots? Color them in!

Color all the shapes that have **u**s in them to find something that helps you get from place to place. One shape has been colored for you.

This is the letter **v**.

Today, Jennifer is watering the tomatoes in her letter garden. Trace or write a **v** on each tomato.

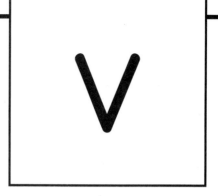

Let's take a trip to the ballpark. What can you see here? Look for all the **v**s hidden in the stadium. Circle each **v** you find.

Hint: There are nine of them.

*Look, one **v** has been circled for you.*

LET'S REVIEW

Help the firefighters fill in the letters **t, u,** and **v** on the rungs of the ladder. First trace the letters, then write them in the same order as the letters you traced.

LET'S REVIEW

Here's a rainbow made of the letters **q, r, s, t, u,** and **v**! Find each of these letters on the alphabet chart. Say each one out loud. Then use the color chart to color in the rainbow.

q = red	t = green
r = orange	u = blue
s = yellow	v = violet

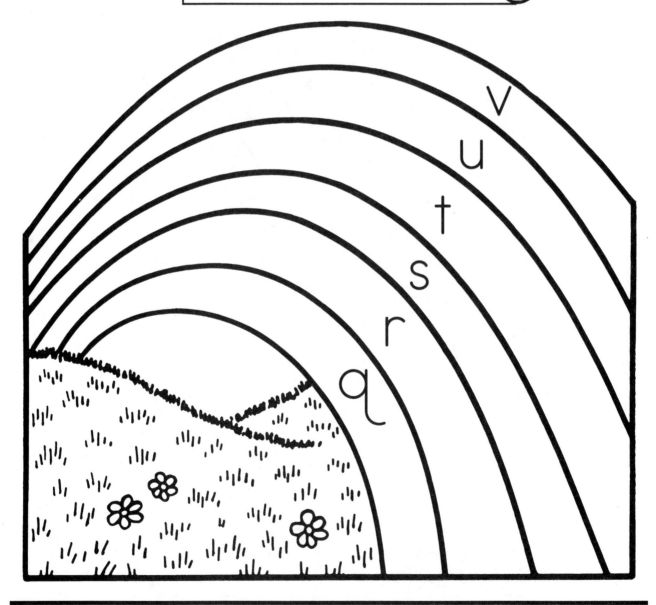

This is the letter **w**.

Andrew is decorating his chocolates with **w**s. Help him by tracing or writing **w**s on each piece of chocolate in the candy box.

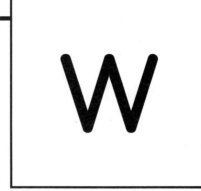

The chocolates in this box have lots of different letters on them. Put an X on all the **w**s you see.

Look, one X has been drawn for you.

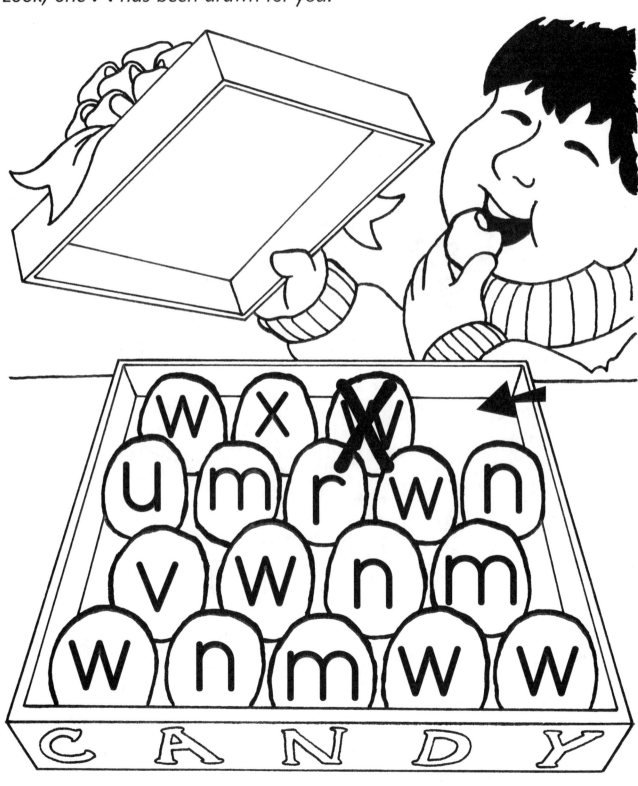

LET'S REVIEW

Today, Heather is measuring Katie's height. This time, they are using a letter ruler that starts with **l** and ends with **w**. Write in the missing letters. Start at the bottom of the ladder and write the letters in order up to the top.

Hint: Look at your alphabet chart if you need help.

What letter shows how tall Katie is?

This is the letter **x**.

Justin has knocked open a piñata full of letter candies. Trace or write an **x** on all the candies you see.

The candies that fell out of the piñata have lots of different letters on them. Circle all the **x**s you see.

*Look, one **x** has been circled for you.*

LET'S REVIEW

Color the shapes that have **w**s and **x**s in them to see what's inside Alex's lunch box. Two shapes have been colored for you.

This is the letter y.

Kelly is practicing writing her name. Help her by tracing or writing in the letter y.

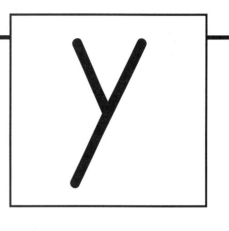

Here is a fun song you might already know. Sing it out loud. Then circle all the ys you see.

Look, one y has been circled for you.

If ⓨou're happy and you know it,
  Clap your hands.

If you're happy and you know it,
  Clap your hands.

If you're happy and you know it,
Then your face will surely show it.

If you're happy and you know it,
  Clap your hands.

This is the letter **z**.

Sam just put on his brand-new letter pajamas. Trace or write a **z** on each polka dot on his pajamas.

z

Timothy and Erin also bought some new letter pajamas. There are many different letters on their pajamas. Draw an X on all the zs you see.

Look, one X has been drawn for you.

LET'S REVIEW

You can make letter music by filling in the letters on each key on the piano. First trace the letters **w, x, y,** and **z** in order. Then write them in the same order on the lines.

LET'S REVIEW

Here's the letter caterpillar again! This time it begins with l and goes all the way to z. Fill in the missing letters. Make sure the letters are in the correct order.

When you are finished, you can use the alphabet chart to check your answers.

LET'S REVIEW

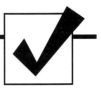

We have learned all of the letters of the alphabet from **a** to **z**. Let's see how much you can remember. Begin with the letter **a** and draw from dot to dot until you reach the letter **z**. What picture have you created? There are more dot-to-dots on the next few pages.

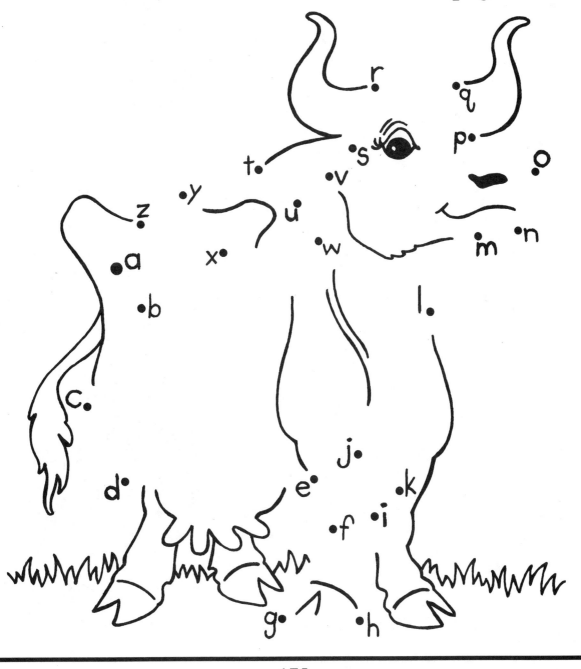

LET'S REVIEW

Begin with the letter **a** and draw from dot to dot until you reach the letter **z**. What kind of picture have you made?

What lowercase letters are in your name?

LET'S REVIEW

Begin with the letter **a** and draw from dot to dot until you reach the letter **z**. What kind of picture have you created?

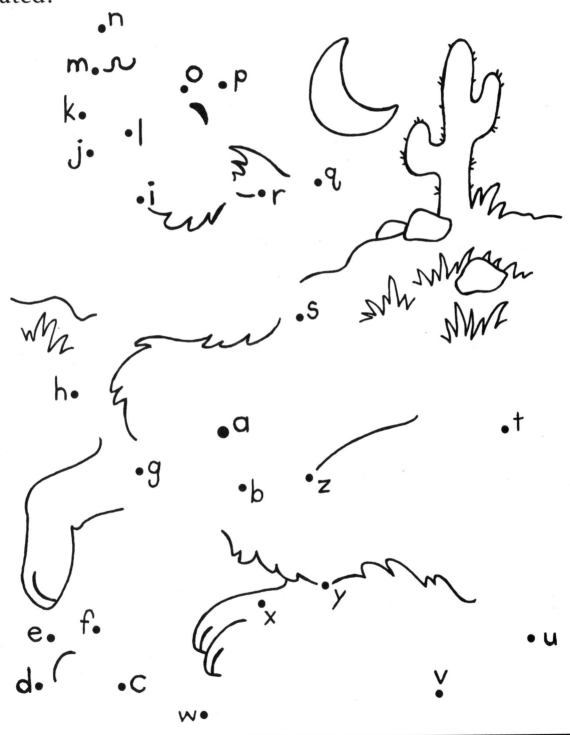

177

LET'S REVIEW

Fill in the letter that comes next in each row. Use the alphabet chart to check your answers.

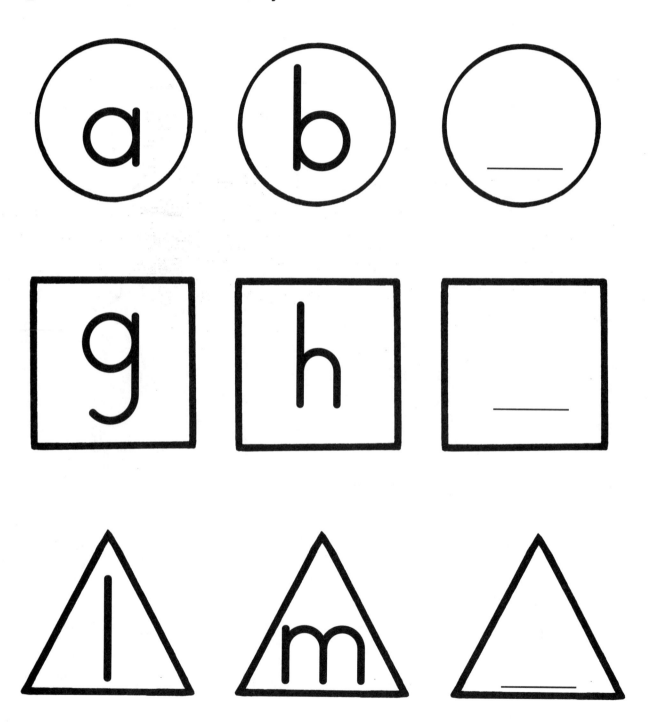

LET'S REVIEW

Fill in the letter that comes next in each row. Use the alphabet chart to check your answers.

LET'S REVIEW

Fill in the letter that comes next in each row. Use the alphabet chart to check your answers.

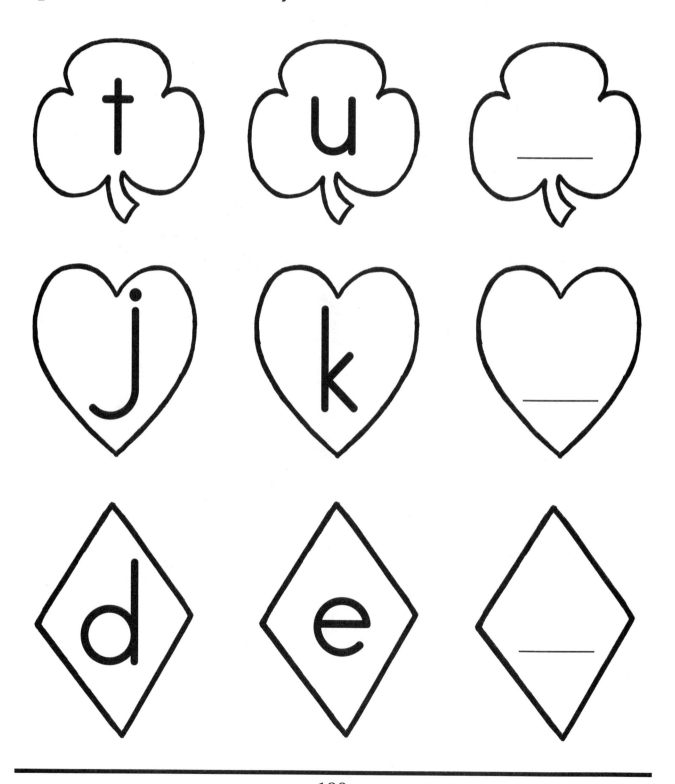

LET'S REVIEW

Fill in the letter that comes first in each row. Use the alphabet chart to check your answers.

181

LET'S REVIEW

Fill in the letter that comes first in each row. Use the alphabet chart to check your answers.

LET'S REVIEW

Fill in the letter that comes first in each row. Use the alphabet chart to check your answers.

COMMON LETTER REVERSALS

On this page and the pages that follow, there are letters that look alike and are sometimes hard to tell apart.

Find all the **b**s on this page and circle them.

*Look, one **b** has been circled for you.*

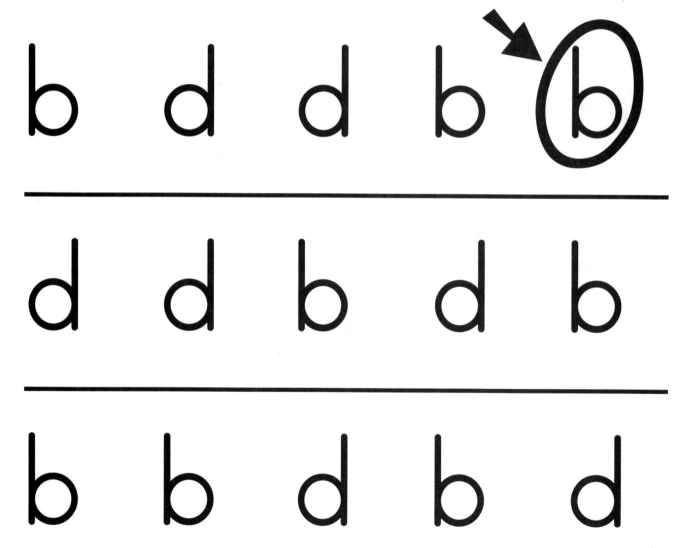

COMMON LETTER REVERSALS

Find all the ds on this page and circle them.

Look, one d has been circled for you.

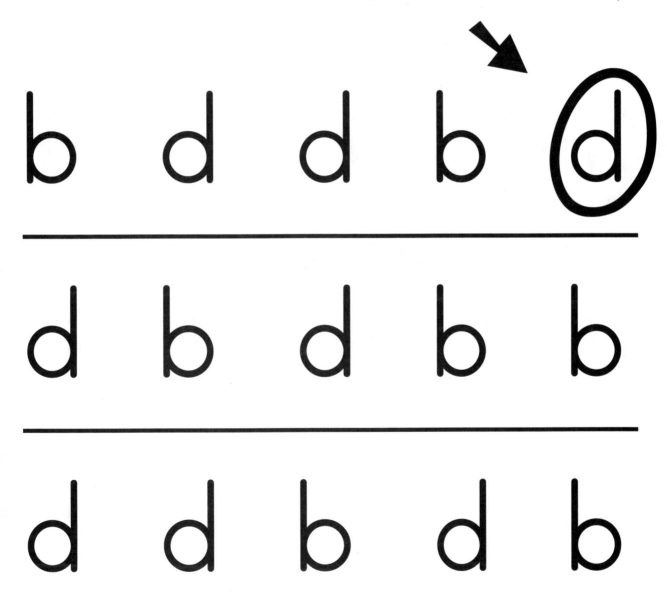

COMMON LETTER REVERSALS

Find all the **g**s on this page and circle them.

Look, one g has been circled for you.

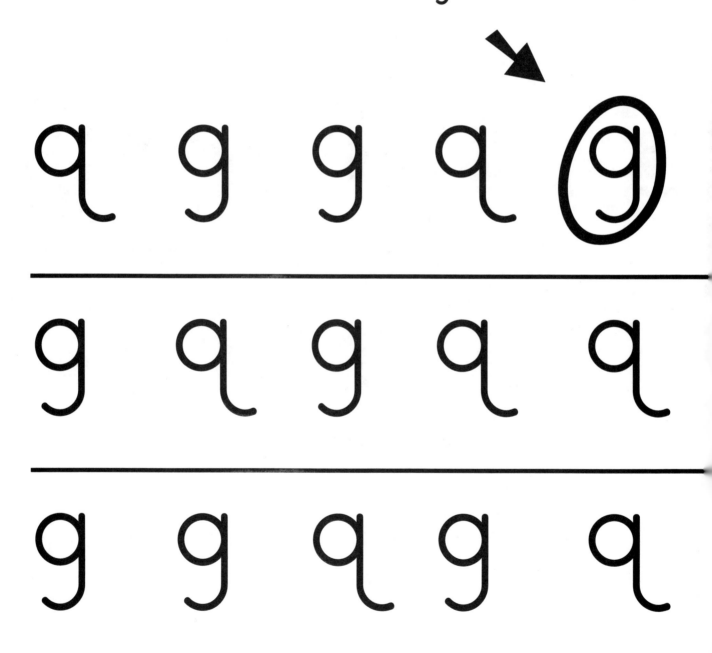

COMMON LETTER REVERSALS

Find all the **q**s on this page and circle them.

*Look, one **q** has been circled for you.*

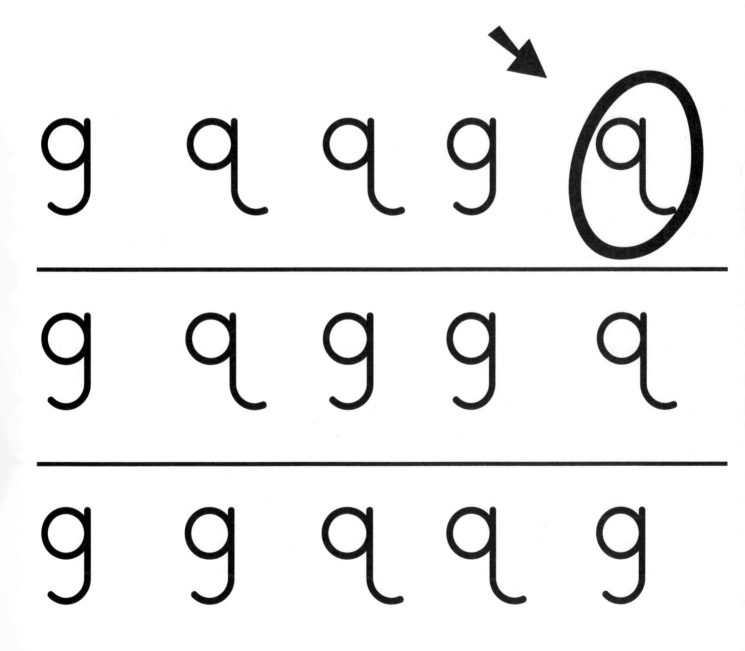

You've really learned a lot about uppercase and lowercase letters. Use the next few pages to practice writing all the letters from Aa to Zz.

Alphabet Chart

a b c d e f g
h i j k l m n
o p q r s t
u v w x y z

HOW TO USE
THIS ALPHABET CHART

This alphabet chart is a reference guide for your child to use and refer to throughout the workbook. It will help your child with the sequencing, recall, and identification of the letters he or she is learning. Do not hesitate to refer to this chart as you move through the exercises. It is good practice for your child to see the letters in relation to one another in their normal place in the alphabet. Seeing letters in this context helps to reinforce your child's learning.

Once your child has become more familiar with the letters, you can use the chart to play letter games with him or her. For example, ask your child, "Can you find the **j**?" If necessary, you can provide helpful hints, such as "It is in the second row." Once your child is ready, increase the difficulty level of the games, asking such questions as, "Can you find the letter that is after **i** and before **k**?"